History's Mysteries

Legends or Lies?

Gary L. Blackwood
with Ruth Siburt

Marshall Cavendish
Benchmark
New York

Marshall Cavendish Benchmark
99 White Plains Road
Tarrytown, NY 10591
www.marshallcavendish.us

Library of Congress Cataloging-in-Publication Data

Blackwood, Gary L.
   Legends or lies? / by Gary L. Blackwood with Ruth Siburt.
    p. cm. — (Benchmark rockets— history's mysteries)
   Includes bibliographical references and index.
   Summary: "Discusses the mysteries surrounding history's legends"—Provided by publisher.
   ISBN 978-0-7614-4359-9
1. Legends—Juvenile literature. 2. Geographical myths—Juvenile literature. I. Siburt, Ruth. II. Title.

GR78.B53 2009
398.209—dc22
2008052759

Publisher: Michelle Bisson
Editorial Development and Book Design: Trillium Publishing, Inc.

Photo research by Trillium Publishing, Inc.

Cover photo: N. C. Wyeth, 1922 (King Arthur); Marie-Lan Nguyen (Amazon warriors stone frieze)

The photographs and illustrations in this book are used by permission and through the courtesy of: *iStockphoto.com*: Ken Pilon (rectangular frame), front cover, back cover, 1, 3, 12, 20, 21; Eliza Snow (oval frame), front cover, 1. *N. C. Wyeth*: 1 (King Arthur), 13. *Marie-Lan Nguyen* (Amazon warriors stone frieze): 1, 10. *Lloyd K. Townsend*: 5. *Corbis*: Bettmann, 6. *Art Resource, NY*: HIP, 8. *James Archer*: 16. *The Granger Collection, New York*: 18, 22. *Cassell's History of England, Century Edition*: 20, 21. *The Bridgeman Art Library International*: Paul Maeyaert, 23. *Sunny Gagliano*: 25. *Claudia Accurso*: 27.

Printed in Malaysia
1 3 5 6 4 2

Contents

Introduction. 4

Chapter One: The Lost Civilization 5

Chapter Two: The Women Warriors 10

Chapter Three: The Lord of Battles 13

Chapter Four: The Outlaw 18

Chapter Five: The City of Gold. 23

Glossary. 28

Find Out More 30

Index 32

Introduction

This is a book about legends. What does this mean? What are legends? How are legends different from myths? How are they different from lies?

Legends are stories passed down from long ago. A legend is supposed to be partly true. It is usually set at a real time and place in history. Both legends and myths may have imaginary characters and events. However, legends focus on human heroes. Myths often focus on gods and goddesses instead. Myths, like legends, are passed down from long ago. Most myths do not have clear historical settings, however. They usually do not even pretend to be factual. Because of this, myths are not legends, but they are also not really lies.

Sometimes a story that people think is a myth turns out to be partly true. For example, people thought the story of the *Iliad* happened in an imaginary city called Troy. Then scientists found the real ruins of this city. Discoveries such as this make people think carefully about which parts of legends and myths are true.

It's a good idea to keep an open mind. Just because a story is written down does not make it true. Also, just because parts of a story seem like fantasy does not make the *whole* story untrue. With this in mind, read on. Decide for yourself: are these stories really legends, myths, or even . . . lies?

CHAPTER ONE

The Lost Civilization

Many legends from around the world tell of great floods that wiped out entire towns or countries. One of the most well-known flood legends is the one about the lost city of Atlantis. Most of what we know comes from the work of a famous Greek writer named **Plato**.

According to legend, the city of Atlantis was very successful and wealthy before it disappeared into the ocean. This painting shows one artist's idea of how it looked.

Around 355 BC, Plato wrote about an island **civilization** that had sunk to the bottom of the Atlantic Ocean in a single day. He said that the name of the place was Atlantis. He also said that he based his flood stories on the writing of a poet who had lived long before him. This poet had heard about Atlantis while visiting Egypt. Plato believed that the stories were real history.

Plato described Atlantis as an amazing city. He said that Atlantis had been created by the Greek god of the sea. The god's son had been the first king of the city. Plato claimed that the island of Atlantis had been bigger than all of Asia. Of course, nobody knew how big Asia was during Plato's time.

Plato also claimed that the people who had lived on the island had been skilled workers. They had built temples, canals, and bridges. They had made things from gold, silver, and bronze.

Around 10,000 BC, the people of Atlantis got into trouble for being greedy. The gods became angry. To punish the people, the gods decided to destroy Atlantis. They sent huge earthquakes and floods to sink it. In just one day and night, the island disappeared to the bottom of the Atlantic Ocean. Or so Plato says.

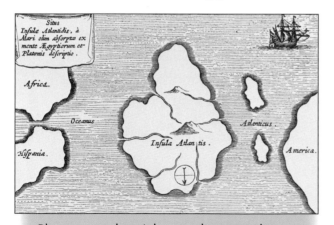

Plato wrote that Atlantis, shown in the center here, had been a giant island civilization in the Atlantic Ocean.

Other **scholars** doubt there ever was an Atlantis. They point out that 10,000 BC was in the Stone Age. No one else on Earth was building canals or working with gold yet. The scholars say that there was never an island as big as Plato said Atlantis was.

Also, the claim that a Greek god made the city is hard for scholars to believe.

Still, many people *do* believe that Atlantis was real. How else, they say, could its legend have survived for thousands of years?

One of the most interesting Atlantis believers was Edgar Cayce. Cayce lived from 1877 to 1945. He claimed that he had special powers. Cayce did "life readings" for people to help them solve problems. He said that during these readings he met more than seven hundred people who had lived past lives in Atlantis. He said he learned about Atlantis from them.

Cayce described Atlantis as being even more **advanced** than Plato had described. Cayce said that people from Atlantis had used submarines. They had flown airplanes. They had watched television. They had even had a special way to create energy. Cayce said that the ruins of Atlantis were off the coast of Florida. He predicted that, in 1968 or 1969, Atlantis would be rediscovered.

Imagine the excitement when, in 1968, divers found a building that looked like a temple off of Florida's coast. It was where Cayce had said Atlantis was! Divers also found what they believed to be a road under water. They wondered: could this be the lost city?

The excitement did not last long. The temple turned out to be a building that divers had used to store things. The "road" was actually a natural rock formation.

Cayce had said that Atlantis was near Florida. Many other people had long felt it was somewhere in the Greek islands. In 1901 a scientist working on the island of Crete found signs of an advanced civilization. More signs of the same civilization were found later on the nearby island of Thera.

The civilization seems to have vanished suddenly around 1500 BC. Some scientists believe a volcano wiped it out. They believe the volcano blew Thera apart and created a wall of water that flooded Crete. Could this have been the basis for the legend of Atlantis?

An ancient eruption blew away most of the Greek island of Thera. This may have been the actual event that led to the legend of Atlantis.

There are problems with the idea that Atlantis was in the Greek islands. The Atlantis that Plato described existed ten thousand years before he lived. However, Thera's volcano erupted only one thousand years before Plato's time. Also, Plato said that Atlantis was in the Atlantic Ocean. Thera and Crete are in the Mediterranean Sea. Finally, neither Thera nor Crete comes close to the size of the island that Plato described.

Still, it is possible the legend of Atlantis is true. Or at least part of it could be. Plato may have recorded some of the details incorrectly. The poet that Plato relied on could have misunderstood the story he heard in Egypt. Or parts of the story may have been **mistranslated**. So, the disappearance of an amazing civilization might still have been real. A giant flood *could* have been the cause for this disappearance.

Perhaps one day we will know for sure. Until then, the lost city of Atlantis will remain a mystery. ❈

CHAPTER TWO

The Women Warriors

This carving shows a Greek soldier battling a woman on a horse. The carving is from the fourth century BC.

The Amazons were legendary woman warriors. For many years, scholars thought that the stories about the Amazons were just Greek myths. Then they found signs that the Amazons may have been real.

Much of what we know about the Amazons *does* come from the Greeks. The Greek poet **Homer** told about "Amazons, who go to war like men." Also, a story about the Greek hero **Heracles** tells how he was forced to steal a **girdle** from an Amazon queen. Heracles came home with the girdle. He also captured some Amazons and brought them home with him.

According to the legend, the Amazons that Heracles left behind joined forces with another group of people called the Scythians. Then these two groups declared war on Greece. The Greeks won this war even though the warrior women fought fiercely.

Another Greek scholar says that the Amazons who were captured by Heracles later escaped. They then fought the Scythians. Eventually they made peace and married the Scythian men. However, this happened only after the men promised that the Amazons could keep hunting and waging war.

Still another scholar wrote about evidence that the Amazons had been in Greece. He said that the names of some places in Greece showed that the Amazons had been there. He said there were graves marking where they had fought.

As time passed, stories about the Amazons got wilder. For example, the Amazons supposedly hated men so much that they mistreated their own male children. Also, they were said to have burned off their right breasts in order to shoot bows better.

As the stories grew wilder, scholars became more doubtful. People thought the Greeks had made up the stories. They thought that women might have fought along with men in some places. However, they did not think there had ever been an entire race of warrior women.

Then, in the late 1800s, people began finding proof. A Russian scholar discovered spears, knives, and arrowheads inside warrior graves. That did not seem unusual. However, most of the warrior skeletons were female.

Since those first skeleton discoveries, other graves of woman warriors have been found. Some of the skeletons have battle wounds. One still had an arrowhead stuck in its skull.

The Amazons and the Scythians were said to have traveled a thousand miles away from the first burial site. Another burial site was discovered there, too. One-fourth of the graves at the site had female skeletons and weapons.

These discoveries have made people rethink the legend of the Amazons. One American scientist, Jeannine Davis-Kimball, said that these women rode in their saddles with "bows and arrows ready to defend their animals, pastures, and clan." There might be something to the stories about the Amazons. It seems that even some experts now think that parts of the woman warrior legend may be real. ✺

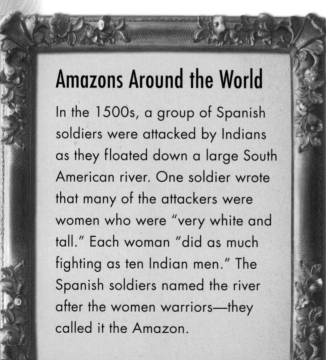

Amazons Around the World

In the 1500s, a group of Spanish soldiers were attacked by Indians as they floated down a large South American river. One soldier wrote that many of the attackers were women who were "very white and tall." Each woman "did as much fighting as ten Indian men." The Spanish soldiers named the river after the women warriors—they called it the Amazon.

CHAPTER THREE

The Lord of Battles

This illustration shows Arthur as a king in battle armor.

King Arthur is among the most admired heroes from any legend. There is a good reason for this. It's hard not to like a leader who earned the trust of his brave knights. According to the legends, Arthur made sure his followers stuck to a strict honor code. He fought dragons. He won a pretty maiden's heart. He pulled a giant sword from a stone. In his kingdom, the sun always shone, legends said.

What parts of the legends were true, though? Many historians think there may be more make-believe than fact in the Arthur legends that we know.

Most books and films present Arthur as if he lived in the twelfth or thirteenth century AD. Historians, however, believe that the real Arthur lived much earlier. That is, if there was a real Arthur at all.

The Arthur story we know today came mostly from a teacher and churchman named Geoffrey of Monmouth. Geoffrey wrote *The History of the Kings of Britain* around the year 1135 AD. As it turns out, this "history" may have been mostly fictional. The book told about Arthur as a knight in shining armor. However, there were no knights like this at the time when Arthur most likely lived. The book also added magical features to Arthur's tale. It told of the wizard Merlin. It told of the mysterious isle of Avalon, where the dying Arthur was taken. Geoffrey said that his stories came from a "very ancient book." Yet there is no record that this book ever existed.

In fact, there are only a few records about Arthur from before Geoffrey's time. Arthur's name first appears in a poem from around 600 AD. Around the time this poem appeared, royal families also began to name their sons Arthur. So it seems likely that Arthur lived sometime before 600 AD.

One text tells about a leader named Arthur who helped defend Britain around this time. The text does not say that this Arthur was a king. Instead it says that Arthur fought "with the Kings of the Britons" against invaders known as the **Saxons**.

This tale fits with history. Experts know for certain that the Britons were fighting the Saxons by the fifth and sixth centuries AD. Just before this, the two groups had worked together. The Saxons had helped the Britons fight other enemies. The Britons had given the Saxons land in return. Then, however, the Saxons had decided they wanted all of the Britons' land. In 442 AD, the Saxons attacked. Suddenly, the Britons were in danger of losing their country.

It was at this point that the leader Artorius, or *Arthur*, arose to save them. This leader became the "lord of battles." He and his men may have begun fighting on horseback, which was a key advantage. The Saxons fought on foot. At the important battle of Mount Badon, around 500 AD, Arthur and his men crushed the Saxons. One historical text said that "nine hundred and sixty men fell . . . from a single charge of Arthur's."

Some legends tell that a magical ship arrived to carry Arthur away from his final battle, to a heavenly place called Avalon. There are many questions, though, about whether the historical records prove when Arthur lived and died. In this painting, three queens care for Arthur as his ship approaches.

The Saxons were badly beaten. They were not finished, however. Thirty years after the battle of Mount Badon, Arthur fought and defeated the Saxons again. This time, though, he lost his life.

Or did he?

An important record from the tenth century AD says that Arthur died fighting the Saxons in 537 AD. (The record also says that his legendary enemy, Mordred, died in the same battle.) In the writings of the twelfth century, however, Arthur did *not* die. Instead, he was taken away to the magical isle of Avalon. According to some legends, Arthur is still resting in Avalon. The legends say he is waiting for a time when Britain needs him again.

At one time, there may have been more evidence about the part of the legend dealing with Arthur's death. In 1190 AD, monks at the Glastonbury Abbey church in southwest England made an important find. It was a skeleton. It was larger than most, and it was in an oak coffin. A lead cross found beneath the coffin had these carved words: "Here lies buried . . . King Arthur in the isle of Avalon." Unfortunately, the abbey was later broken into. Arthur's skeleton disappeared.

The carving on the cross was strange for a few reasons. First, the Arthur that people had written about had not been a king. So it was odd that the words on the cross said that he was. Second, Glastonbury is not an island. At one time, however, the hill that the abbey sits on was surrounded by marshes. That could have made it *seem* like an island.

Then there is the lettering on the cross. It was not the kind of lettering that people used in the twelfth century. Scholars believe the letters were more like those from the sixth century.

The trouble is that *none* of the evidence is completely clear. Was Arthur real? When did he live? Was he a king? When did he die? How much of his legend can be explained by facts? The story of Arthur remains mysterious to this day. ✤

CHAPTER FOUR

The Outlaw

This painting shows Robin Hood and Maid Marian meeting. Their love was one of many things that seem to have been added to Robin's legends over the years.

After King Arthur, Robin Hood is probably the best-known hero of British legends. Robin's adventures have been told many times in many ways. The large number of tellings make it hard to sort out the truth. With each telling, new things seem to have been added.

For example, the earliest stories do not mention Robin's relationship with Maid Marian. They do not say he stole from the rich to give to the poor. Such additions to the legend of Robin Hood make it hard to learn about the real person.

Robin Hood's story likely began seven hundred years after King Arthur's. So there are more written records, which should make it easier to find facts. It doesn't. Instead, the records just give us many confusing choices.

For example, *Robin* may be a nickname for *Robert*. Or *Robin* may be an **alias**. Both of these ideas allow for more men to have been the "Outlaw of Sherwood Forest." Robin's real name could have been anything.

Most scholars think that Robin must have lived before the 1370s. They think this because of a famous poem that appeared at this time. The poem was about someone called Robyn Hode. The scholars believe that Robin must have already been a legend when this poem was written.

The idea that Robin stole from the rich and gave to the poor came from another poem written in the late 1300s. *A Gest* [tale] *of Robin Hood* calls Robin an outlaw who did good things for poor men. This poem is probably fictional. Still, it is a useful source. There may be some truth to it.

The *Gest* presents Robin as a gentleman. A play from the 1500s suggested more. It presented Robin as the Earl of Huntington. Later, in the 1700s, a man named William Stukeley made a family tree for this **earl**, who he said was Robin Hood. Stukeley's work is interesting. However, it is not strong evidence that Robin Hood was an earl, or that he even existed.

People disagree about exactly when Robin Hood lived. The *Gest* poem hints that Robin lived during the rule of King Edward. This does not help much, though. There were three kings named Edward. They ruled at different times over a period of more than one hundred years. Nobody knows which Edward ruled when Robin Hood lived.

Around 1838, a researcher named Joseph Hunter discovered notes about a "Robert Hode" near where Robin Hood is most often said to have lived. The notes say that Robin was fined for not serving in the king's army.

Hunter thought that Hode may have joined a rebel band fighting King Edward II. When the leader of these rebels was captured and killed, many who had fought with him became

Edward I ruled from 1272–1307.

Edward II ruled from 1307–1327.

outlaws. Hode (or Robin Hood) may have been one. It is interesting that the rebels wore the same shade of green that Robin Hood and his men are said to have worn.

According to Hunter, King Edward II went to Sherwood Forest in 1323. This forest is where the legends say that Robin hid. The king went to investigate illegal deer hunting. The *Gest* records this, too. It says that the king pardoned Robin. For one year, Robin became a servant to the king.

Hunter also found several notes about a "Robyn Hode" being paid as a servant of King Edward II. The last record of his pay was November 1324—one year after the king visited Sherwood Forest. This date matches the claims of the *Gest*.

Records say that Robin Hood lived when King Edward ruled England. But which King Edward was it?

Edward III ruled from 1327–1377.

For Hunter and others, these records prove that Robert Hode, Robyn Hode, and Robin Hood were the same man.

Other people disagree. Some believe that Robin Hood lived later. Some think Robin is a mix of many heroes put together. Still others believe Robin is completely fictional. They think writers and poets made him up to give hope to poor people in difficult times.

Whichever idea is right, a few things are certain. The people of the Middle Ages believed in Robin Hood. Ever since then he has been a heroic symbol. Whether his stories were purely legends or part of history, he will be remembered as the outlaw who did good deeds for people in trouble.

In one Robin Hood legend, he shot an arrow out a window from his deathbed to decide where he should be buried.

CHAPTER FIVE

The City of Gold

For many centuries people have been charmed by gold. They have searched for it. They have killed for it. They have died for it. One of the most famous legends of all is about an entire city built of gold. The name of this city is *El Dorado*.

In the 1620s, a Spanish monk wrote about a lake in what is now Colombia, a country in South America. The monk wrote about how the local people used the lake in a **ceremony** to honor their gods. They coated their chief with a sticky tar. Then they sprinkled the chief with gold dust.

The legend of El Dorado began as a story about a man coated in gold and then grew into a story about a whole city of gold. The story of the golden man was probably based on a real Indian ceremony that involved coating a chief in gold dust.

Men then rowed the chief to the middle of the lake. He made an offering to the gods there. He threw emeralds and gold pieces into the water. He washed the gold dust from his body with special herbs. The gold dust fell off his body into the water. That was the end of the ceremony.

The Spanish had been in Central and South America for about one hundred years when the monk wrote down the story. The Spanish were looking for gold. They took as much as they could get from the local people. The Spanish took so much gold that another monk wrote that they worshipped it "as a god."

When a Spanish man named Sebastian Belalcázar heard the story of the chief covered in gold dust, he set out to find the chief's lake (and also conquer new territory). He took hundreds of soldiers with him. He also took along a thousand Indians. He thought it would take about two weeks to find the lake.

Belalcázar did not know it, but two other groups were also looking for the famous lake. The first was led by a man named Gonzalo Jiménez de Quesada. His group of seven hundred men had set out from the coast of what is now Colombia. A German adventurer named Nicolaus Federmann led the other group. It had set out from what is now the country of Venezuela.

This map shows the routes of the three El Dorado explorers and the names today for countries and cities in the area.

Map labels: Barranquilla, Maracaibo, Caracas, Panama City, PANAMA, VENEZUELA, Bogotá, Lake Guatavitá, Cali, COLOMBIA, Quito, ECUADOR, Guayaquil, PERU, BRAZIL

Legend:
Sebastian Belalcázar
Gonzalo Jiménez de Quesada
Nicolaus Federmann

It was a hard trip for all three groups. It rained so much that their clothes rotted. They had to hack their way through thick jungles. Mosquitoes and snakes bit them. Angry Indians shot at them with poisoned arrows.

Quesada was the first of the three explorers to find the lake. It took him ten months. By the time he got there, he had only 166 men left with him. He *did* find rich people living near the lake. But they had traded salt to get the gold they now had.

There was no doubt, though, that Quesada had found the right lake. The people there had in the past coated their chiefs in gold dust and rowed them out on the lake. They just had not done this for many years.

Quesada was disappointed, but he claimed the area for Spain anyway. He made it into a new kingdom. Then he built a church (which was the beginning of today's city of Bogotá, Colombia).

Meanwhile, it took Belalcázar more than two *years* to reach the lake. This was much longer than the two *weeks* he had predicted. His army was also down to 166 men. When they arrived, they were upset to see that Quesada had beaten them.

Federmann's group arrived even later. His group had also (amazingly) been reduced to 166 men. Oddly enough, the leaders who had worked so hard to find the lake didn't stay long. All three men soon decided to head home.

Quesada left his brother Hernán in charge. Hernán had men empty the large lake with small, hollow **gourds**. He found four thousand pieces of gold at the bottom. This seemed like a lot. Still, it was not El Dorado. Hernán searched for the golden city somewhere else.

Another man named Gonzalo Pizarro went looking for El Dorado in 1541. Pizarro used torture to try to force people to tell him where El Dorado was. One clever Indian chief got around this problem. He gave Pizarro false directions to El Dorado that led Pizarro far away. In this way, the chief and his people stayed safe.

Pizarro failed to find the city of gold. However, that did not stop others from trying. The search went on. Men spent years looking. They gave up their lives. But still, no one ever found El Dorado. The story of this giant city of gold is one more legend that has—so far—not lived up to the stories people told. ✳

This copper and gold treasure was one of the pieces found in the lake (known now as Lake Guatavitá). It shows the chief being rowed on the lake during the ceremony of the golden man.

advanced: Developed beyond an early or basic level.

alias: A name used instead of a real name to keep the real name secret.

ceremony: A set of activities that honor a special time, event, person, or god.

civilization: An organized society or group of people with its own beliefs and laws.

earl: A British nobleman.

girdle: A piece of clothing, or in some cases armor, that people wear around the waist.

gourds: Round containers made from dried-out squash-like plants.

Heracles: A god-man in Greek mythology. Heracles was given a set of seemingly impossible tasks. He is also known as Hercules in Roman mythology.

Homer: (born about 700 BC) A Greek poet credited with the original tellings of the *Iliad* and the *Odyssey*, probably in the eighth or ninth century BC. Many people believe the poems were recited aloud long before anyone wrote them down.

mistranslated: Incorrectly changed from one language to another language.

Plato: (about 428–347 BC) A famous Greek writer who studied philosophy and politics. He taught another famous Greek scholar—Aristotle.

Saxons: Members of a group of tribes from what is now northern Germany. The Saxons invaded England in the fifth century AD.

scholars: People who study things deeply.

Find Out More

Books

Blackwood, Gary L. *Legends or Lies?* New York: Marshall Cavendish, 2006.

For readers who would like to know more about legends and lies, this book has more detail.

DeMolay, Jack. *Atlantis: The Mystery of the Lost City.* New York: PowerKids Press, 2007.

This highly illustrated book contains brief discussions of what Atlantis was like and where it might have been located.

White, T. H. *The Once and Future King.* (Reprint) Temecula, CA: Textbook Publishers, 2003.

This is a reprint of a classic collection of King Arthur tales. The stories follow Arthur from when he was a young boy through his legendary adventures as a king.

Websites

**http://www.activemind.com/Mysterious/Topics/
Atlantis**
This site introduces basic information about the Atlantis
legend. It links to translations of Plato's work and other
articles about Atlantis.

**http://www.bbc.co.uk/history/british/middle_ages/
robin_01.shtml**
This British Broadcasting Corporation (BBC) site has a
summary of the Robin Hood legend and its history.

**http://www.pbs.org/wnet/secrets/previous_seasons/
case_amazon**
This *Secrets of the Dead* case file from the Public
Broadcasting Service (PBS) provides an overview of the
legends about Amazon warriors. It also links to other
resources and interactive features.

http://www.public.iastate.edu/~camelot/arthur.html
This site links to many other sites about King Arthur.

Index

Page numbers for photographs and illustrations are in **boldface**.

Amazons (women warriors),
  10, 10–12
Arthur, King, **13**, 13–17, **16**
Atlantis, **5**, 5–9, **6**
Avalon, isle of, 14, 16, 17

Belalcázar, Sebastian, 24, 26

Cayce, Edgar, 7–8
Crete (Greek island), 8, 9

Davis-Kimball, Jeannine, 12

Edward I, **20**
Edward II, **20**, 20–21
Edward III, **21**
El Dorado, **23**, 23–27, **27**

Federmann, Nicolaus, 24, 26

Geoffrey of Monmouth, 14
Glastonbury Abbey, 17

Heracles, 10, 11
Homer, 10
Hunter, Joseph, 20–21

Maid Marian, 18, **18**
Merlin, 14
Middle Ages, 22

Pizarro, Gonzalo, 26, 27
Plato, 5–7, 9

Quesada, Gonzalo
  Jiménez de, 24, 25, 26
Quesada, Hernán, 26

Robin Hood, **18**, 18–22, **22**

Saxons, 15–16
Scythians, 10, 11, 12
Sherwood Forest, 19, 21

Thera (Greek island), 8, **8**, 9
treasure, **27**